Pet Care

Fish for You

Caring for Your Fish

Written by Susan Blackaby   Illustrated by Charlene DeLage

Content Adviser: Jennifer Zablotny, D.V.M.

Reading Adviser: Susan Kesselring, M.A., Literacy Educator

Rosemount-Apple Valley-Eagan (Minnesota) School District

PICTURE WINDOW BOOKS

Editor: Nadia Higgins
Designer: Nathan Gassman
Page production: Picture Window Books
The illustrations in this book were painted with watercolor.

Picture Window Books
5115 Excelsior Boulevard
Suite 232
Minneapolis, MN 55416
1-877-845-8392
www.picturewindowbooks.com

Printed in the United States of America.
1 2 3 4 5 6 08 07 06 05 04 03

Library of Congress Cataloging-in-Publication Data
Blackaby, Susan.
Fish for you : caring for your fish / written by Susan Blackaby ; illustrated by Charlene DeLage.
v. cm. — (Pet care)
Contents: Finding out about fish—Cold-water fish—Warm-water fish—Setting up an aquarium—Getting your
supplies—Ready, set, fish!—Taking care of your fish—Fish world—Fun facts—Goldfish guide.
ISBN 1-4048-0116-2 (lib. bdg.)
1. Aquarium fishes—Juvenile literature. [1. Fish as pets.] 1. DeLage, Charlene, 1944- ill. II. Title.
SF457.25 .B58 2003
639.34—dc21
2002155001

TABLE OF CONTENTS

Finding Out About Fish

Most of the earth is covered by water.

A world of amazing fish is hidden beneath that water.

How can you learn about these fish?

Read library books. Go snorkeling. Visit a zoo's aquarium.

Set up a home aquarium and study fish up close.

Cold-water Fish

Some fish live in cold water.

They are the easiest fish to care for.

They can live in a pond or a bowl.

Goldfish are cold-water fish.

Goldfish come in lots of shapes and sizes.

Some wiggle and waddle. Some dart and scoot.

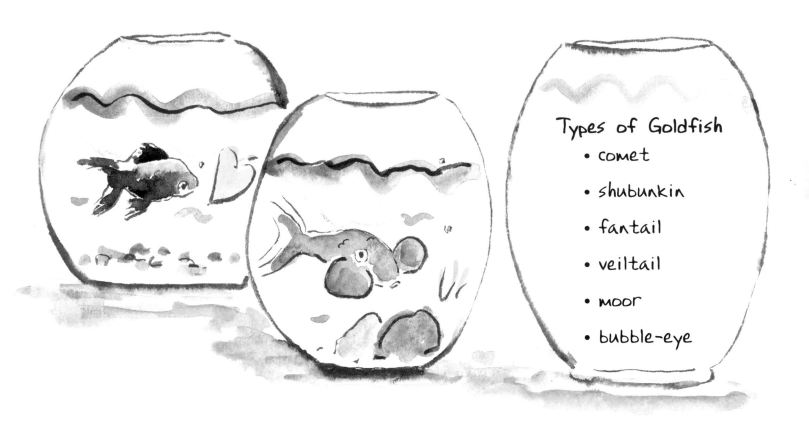

Types of Goldfish
- comet
- shubunkin
- fantail
- veiltail
- moor
- bubble-eye

Warm-water Fish

Some fish need to live in warm water.

They are called tropical fish.

You need to set up an aquarium for them.

Most kinds of tropical fish are peaceful,
but some don't get along with other types of fish.
It is important to choose fish that can live together happily.

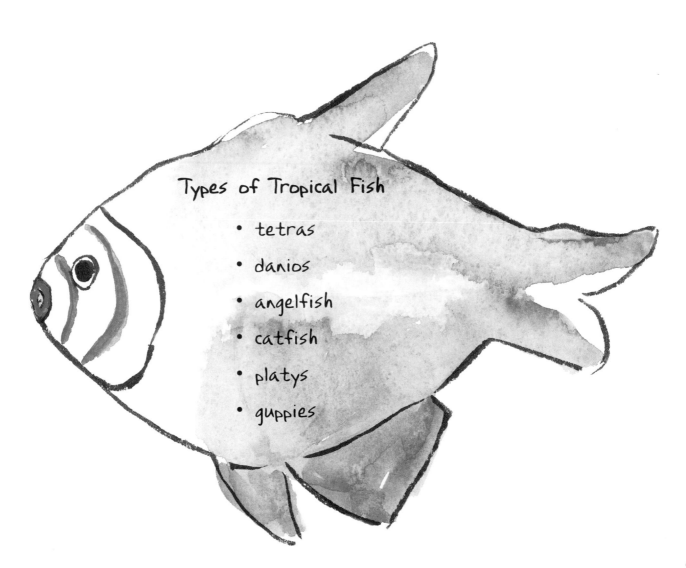

Types of Tropical Fish

- tetras
- danios
- angelfish
- catfish
- platys
- guppies

Setting Up an Aquarium

You will need a clear tank so you can see your fish.

Use a tank that can hold 10 or 20 gallons of water.

Your fish won't be happy if the tank is too crowded.

A 10-gallon tank can hold 10 small fish.

Or, a 10-gallon tank can hold 5 medium-sized fish.

Fish Size Guide

- 10 gallons (38 liters) holds
  10 fish that are 1 inch (2½ cm) long.

- 10 gallons (38 liters) holds
  5 fish that are 2 inches (5 cm) long.

Find a sturdy place to put your tank.

You won't be able to move it when it is full of water.

Do not put the aquarium in a sunny spot.

Getting Your Supplies

You will need clean gravel for the bottom of the tank.

Plants, rocks, and fun things will give your fish places to hide.

An air pump and a water filter will help keep the water clean.

You will need a heater to keep the water warm.
Find out how warm the water needs to be for the
fish you choose. Check the temperature of the water
to make sure it is just right for your fish.

You will need a lid to keep the fish from jumping out.

A light will help you see their bright colors.

Don't leave the light on all the time. Your fish need rest, too.

Ready, Set, Fish!

Start slowly. Set the aquarium up and fill it with water. Don't add any fish right away. Let the air pump and filter work, and add a few flakes of fish food each day.

After two weeks, your aquarium will be ready for fish.

FOOD

16

Add only two fish each week.

Your fish will come home from the store in a plastic bag.

Let the bag rest in the water tank for a half hour.

Then let the fish swim into their new home.

Things to Remember

• Choose fish that can live together.

• Add fish only after you have fed the old fish.

• Add fish when the tank is dark.

Taking Care of Your Fish

Feed your fish a little bit of food two or three times a day.

Do not feed your fish too much!

Too much food makes

the tank messy.

To keep the water fresh, you will need to change some of it each week. Always let tap water sit for a few days before you add it.

Keep your aquarium clean.

Use a scrubber to clean the sides of your tank.

Cleaning helps keep the fish healthy.

Cleaning lets you see into their world.

You can watch your fish dart and swim.

They will be happy in the home you have made for them.

Fish World

What is it like at the bottom of the sea? Get a big sheet of paper. Draw an underwater world. You can add sea creatures, rocks, plants, treasure chests, and mermaids. Then tape your picture to the back of your aquarium.

Fun Facts

- Japanese koi are goldfish. They can be three feet (almost one meter) long!
- Goldfish can live to be 20 years old.
- Baby fish are called fry.
- A group of fish is called a school.
- Fish do not have eyelids.
- Fish use their gills to breathe. The gills take oxygen out of the water.

Words to Know

air pump—a small machine that blows air bubbles through water

aquarium—a see-through tank of water where fish live

filter—a special strainer for cleaning water

gravel—small pieces of rock

Goldfish Guide

There are lots of kinds of goldfish.

This chart tells you about a few of them.

What is its name?	What does it look like?
Comet	A comet is slim with long fins.
Shubunkin	A shubunkin is spotted.
Fantail	A fantail is chubby with two tail fins.
Veiltail	A veiltail has fins like a long scarf.
Moor	A moor is black with long fins.
Bubble-eye	A bubble-eye has a bulge under each eye.

To Learn More

At the Library

Frost, Helen. *Fish*. Mankato, Minn.: Pebble Books, 2001.

Morley, Christine and Carole Orbell. *Me and My Pet Fish*. Chicago: World Book in association with Two-Can, 1997.

Walker, Pamela. *My Goldfish*. New York: Children's Press, 2001.

On the Web

ASPCA Kids' Site
http://www.animaland.org
For stories, games, and information about pets

Goldfish Society
http://www.goldfishsociety.org
For information on goldfish and goldfish care

Want to learn more about fish?
Visit FACT HOUND at *http://www.facthound.com*.

Index